Lit Soul:

My Journey Back to Faith.

By Jessi Hersey

<u>Copyright</u>

All content @copyright 2020 Onenesslove Publishing LLC

All rights reserved.

No part of this book may be used without written permission by Author.

www.1nesslove.com

ISBN:978-1-7362381-9-6

Illustrated by: Helena Gottberg

Written by: Jessi Hersey

Edited by: Victoria Jo and Maritza Mendoza

About the Book

Lit Soul: My Journey back to faith is a collection of poetry written in four sections about love, loss, finding your place in the world, and coming back to what you can't see, which is faith. It's an honest telling of poet Jessi's life from the age of 6 years old to the present day. It's having faith again and growing it stronger through each section. It's a place to find that we aren't so different after all. Each poem sheds light on ideas and concepts we deal with every day, from the pandemic to black lives matter. If you are an avid reader that loves poetry, this book is for you

POET'S BIO

Born in Bakersfield, California only to move to Colorado. Where she got a BA in psychology but began writing poetry when she was 6 years old. She is an Author, Publishing processes Coach, founder of her publishing company, and school Onenesslove publishing. She is a blogger on medium and writes about education, self-love, and living life to the fullest. She loves helping others through writing. She is currently learning how to write the music for her own music production. She has many stories to come.

<u>Thank you</u>

First, I want to thank God for always being in my life even when I refused to accept that and for

loving me unconditionally through it. I want to thank my family for always standing by me even when I couldn't see that. I want thank my close friend Katy Vargo thank you for believing in me and loving me through everything I wrote and being my biggest fan of my writing. This is an updated version of my original poetry and it's not in order of when each poem was written but the order of the meaning and the path, I took to better understand myself and other. You will find poems I wrote for and about others. To me making sense of the world is through writing. Poetry in essence is a spiritual experience alone. You go deep within to all those places and feeling your sometimes afraid to go and you go. In my original poetry book, I talked about love and God. In this one I still do and I am still a proud member of the LGBTQ community but if I were to label my love, I love both men and women. I am exploring further my own sexuality and feelings. My faith in God has grown stronger and I thank him for every blessing in my life and that I have a loving and forgiving family.

I thank him for always showing me the way and allowing me to take off the masks of others as I no longer wear one. These poems are my truth and my journey through finding myself again. Learning to love that little girl that wrote some of these poems and to love the adult I have become. To know that love is real and available to everyone.

8/24/19

Dear God,

Thank you for blessing me with the gift of always being protected and guided every step of the way and leading me to my heart's desire no matter what it looked like on the outside. You were always there loving me passionately and comforting me in my time of need, you welcomed people in my path unexpectedly from soul sister to divine brothers and sisters coming together to help me see how loved I am by you and supporting me. You taught me to never give up on myself even if on the outside it looked like the world was ending that was just the illusion. You were really just making room for the new life and energy entering into each stage of my life never leaving my side.

The truth is you never left and your still are here loving me and teaching me love. I surrender to your loving embrace and powerful divine love. You are my creator and I am your perfect divine child. This poetry is my story to everyone to all your children. To see their divine truth and help in guiding them in their creative juices flowing. I love you God you are my everything, my lover and partner in life. You gifted me with a forever person Jay. As we all have twin flames. Thank you for all my blessing from these words of poetry written to the music in my soul wanting to be out and sharing. Sharing you with everyone. As I get to know myself, I get to know you. What a blessing that is and a blessing to be following my heart which is YOU. You're always leading the way thank you God.

I love you,

Jess

Table of Contents

Humanity

God

Following my heart:
The core, the beat, and the magic.
Within the soul,
from the one
who made me whole,
from melting pieces and
an inundated self.
He made me whole,
a Divine form,
only to share

the love,

the gift

that was given

in the written

Word and the peace I

I found in Him.

September 21, 2018

Protector

Echoes of many consuming heartbeats,
proclaim a soul to protect and love,
the lost, homeless, desolate and broken.
Life treats
the protector to a dove
of the heart's unspoken Words.

2015

Life

Dark Brown Eyes are able to see into the Soul,

as the heartbeat of this soul rises,

trying to find what makes herself whole.

Getting lost in time,

in the climb of life,

only to define,

what it means to Love,

and most importantly to love

profoundly,

Even in fear of the unknown:

to forgive,

to see,

to be forgiven,

to embrace

to experience joy,

to live, become, and share

the promises of tomorrow.

To find one's self,

to learn —

only to accept herself with the beauty that exists within.

January 12, 2018

K

Heart as pure as Gold

And honest

Where childhood meet forever

Is a close friend

Like a trend

Ready to share

To what comes natural to the heart

It's the art of being true

To who you are

And always being there

Because you care.

9/19/2020

Fly

Birds gliding in the sky

Eyeing

The ground below

Only to Glow

With the thought

Of home

With God

Who never left

The wings were only growing

To learn God is home.

9/21/2020

The Lost Soul

As the smells of the season
run through the veins,
the thoughts of freedom,
permeates
the mind,
of a lost soul.
A soul, which cannot even see.
Though the illusion isn't what it seems,
the soul is blinded by greed and grief,
yet, what this soul cannot see,
is that the life in life ahead holds more love,
Then any mortal soul can bring,
that life gifts you the chords of love,
but, slowly, the thought creeps into
the eyes of the lost soul, and there,
a golden dove goes flying into
the ocean sky to be found

January 6, 2006

Beauty

Let those on Earth
be forgiven.
Let those who have been hurt
be healed,
and may those in need
of food, be fed.

Let the ones with hatred
in their hearts transform it into love
and strength, and may the one
with a disability become gifted

with the gifts of life.

May backstabbing change
And help others,
may the worries turn into happiness.
May beauty and image
Look inward and
Not outward.

And for life to not be
looked upon as time lost,
but as time well-spent.
For everyone to be treated as equals,
by the beauty we have within us.

May all the wars stop,
instead of continue.
May the judging stop.
That will be the day,
when hopes and dreams come true.
And our world can indeed be called beautiful.

October 2001

Vietnam

Picking up the pieces
of the deceased,
of the once living and breathing.

The thought of flying
Flows through the veins of a soldier;
A soldier caught in the middle of it all —
Between life and death,
watching friends and loved ones
killed in an instant flip of weapons.

The heart grows weary when seeing death
spread throughout the jungle.
For the death of the mundane
to a soldier's eye after so long of seeing
without any time to mourn —
To mourn those who were killed.

The only thing to spare is hope,
hope for the war to end,
for peace to be our psalm and rhythm,
and for the war to have all been a nightmare.

June 18, 2006

Rose

Dreams of a past that
Washes over a restless mind.
A friend with a dark past who left us in death.
A story of her life,
From the moment we met till the word of her passing,
Yet looking back at the constant memories,
Lays a young woman trying to find her way,
Each step taken lightly,
Friends and Family always running through her mind.
She was an unforgettable person in life and death;
A memorable one.

2008

Christmas Prayer

May your Christmas be filled with family and all the ones you
Love.
May life take you through a journey of hope and give you the
Willpower
To never give-up, even when it seems as though there is no
Hope.
May you learn more and more about your inner
Beauty.
May you follow your heart to wherever it brings you,
May
Your life be filled with all the love a person can
Hold,
All the friends and family person can handle,
All
The faith, hope, and light, a person can only dream of,
And
May you always remember your golden heart that shines
Inside and out.

December 2004

Joan of Arc

The cries of war vibrate through a golden shield.
Behind it, on a white stallion, sits a woman in armor
disguised as a man and she points her sword
to the army that waits below.

A thunderous roar begins the clash.
Blood is lost as brave men die by swords,
their valor caught in time.
The war was won for she heard
She heard God's voice "fight it's a winning battle."
Her destiny is revealed to the people;
she fought and won,
yet the punishment for dressing like a man is death
because it is like being a witch.

For holding on to her belief in God and the saints,
she must take her fate,
stick to what she believes to be true.
Crazy, she is not, even though some may think so.
She is full of devotion,
yet she must burn in the devil's flames
for being a great woman of faith.

2001

When all seems fine

And it's time to dine,
Things begin to come to life
When it's time
For the truth to be revealed
Of who you are
And your intentions
Everything else falls away,
Leaving nothing but space
And time
To grow
And know
Your never alone.

2020

Spiritual River

As the hours pass by slowly, our hearts aches
Of our loved ones leaving only to
Come back when life has changed,
It is both good and bad
There is one question that sticks in mind.
Will it really be both bad and good?
It will
For God is our father and his wish for us is to
Learn pain, hope, love, and most of all to
Come to him in our hard times.
Nobody has to hold in pain or it will come out in horrible ways
So, when you are sobbing in your river try to make
It a spiritual river and remember God is your Father and healer.

2002

Friendship

The beginning of this friendship was new and challenging

With its bumps and turns

It was forever changing.

From each other

Whether for better or worst

We seemed to find the best within each other

Like a constant thirst.

Now that we are older

This friendship has become new again.

Like a grain of sand that becomes a hill of sand

Our friendship grows with every step.

Each footstep embeds a solid footprint in the sand
A print of friendship that will forever be remembered
Whenever it may lead us or
Whatever journey may fall upon us.

1999

When

When will the tears
of fear and sadness fade away?
When will we see the brightness of the day?
And when will we sing a new song?

Shall we spend our lives in sorrow,
instead of with a heart filled with
With loads of happiness?

Can we ever see the one star
that comes falling and calling to give us,
forgiveness and love?
A star that conquers our hopes and dreams
and helps us believe in who we are.
We are filled with questions of 'when' but
the star looks and echoes to us, 'it is now.'

January 2002

Manic Mind

You look in a mirror
watching a person who looks like you
but doesn't act like you.
Who is this creature?
Who swallows pills as if it were candy?
Who is this person,
who tries to control
rational thoughts?
This isn't you!
It was never you, and never would be.
You would never take your life,
whoever it is, taking
those lifeless little white pills
is taking you with them.
They're taking you through the dark tunnel of frustration,
futility, then death.

Sleep comforts you and for a split second.
You feel normal.
You feel in control of your wild emotions,
Body split, numbness and emptiness,
Again, you feel in control of your wild emotions,
That go up and down like a see-saw,
Never knowing where you're headed next.

Your eyelids are feeling heavier.

Even though your eyes are already shut, there is

A sparkle of light coming between the bright darkness.

The sensation of a heartbeat that kept

you alive has stopped.

Could this be the place everyone had dreamed about?

No, it's you dying a slow death.

But when the end is met, the madness will be gone.

Only goodness and rest will take its place

November 6, 2009

Your Daughter

*A piece dedicated to my 8th grade teacher who lost her daughter to
cancer.*

Since your heart can't take away the pain
of the one you love and lost,
the loss still follows you like a shadow,
and you feel you can't do anything about it,
yet there yet there is a pathway to comfort and peace.

It is to remember, but with remembrance comes memory.
It is to remember your daughter was brought to life by you
and she is now a part of you that is alive.
She is in your heart,
Telling you she loves you with her whispers,
As she navigates a place of wonders and joy
where there is beauty and light,
where there is grace and tranquility.
She is in the hands of her heavenly father
who loves you and your daughter equally.

Life never ends, and so her love will never end,
and neither will your love for her.
That is the beautiful thing about life,
your daughter lives on.

March 4, 2003

Pandemic

Sitting in time alone
To get back
To finding our
True self
In a time that seems filled with fear
Though fear is the nothing
Peace is what is real
God
Guiding us all back
To ourselves
To Him
To our father
God

4/26/2020

Day Break

Light from the Moon shines down
On a small town in darkness
Making it a little lighter
When it's time for sunrise
The innocent will wake and love will shine
Spreading through the town like a river.
Passing by for just a moment
A little moment
With many more to come

2005

Black and White

These are constructed lies
society told us to tie
the bonds of racism tighter with...
to make each fighter
from within rise to the occasion
of equality among people,
people that are part of the
Human race
because as human we are laced with flaws
that can lead to tragedy or applause.
but we are one in this mortal
plane of existence,
We must not see black or white
But all as one,
completely whole.

2015

Forceful Injustice

The penetration against
the unwilling body.
Skin shivers, life freezes
only to begin again
once the act
of taking away
what was thought
to be loving
now leaves of aftermath of terror,
with the thought of hope
that it was only a nightmare.
If only it were true,
the will to find a way back
is promising and
with that, there
are endless possibilities
January 6, 2012

Consequence

Unexpected and Blind
Justice, the trick of the game,
to disguise
what was once innocent
into a toy that's
the perpetrator is holding strings.
The protective shield shattered
what was taught fallen
in a moment of shame,
this disgusting
excuse for a human has the strings,
yet, the power is still within
the survivor's hands,
cutting
the restrains...
Fighting towards Freedom!
2012

The Abused

Wrinkles cover a warned down life

who had lived to exist

in a world of strife,

where a

f – i – s – t

was continually being thrown.

As the ages passed,

The abuser is a wayfarer, their homes

are the faces of the abused,

They're left as empty shells;

The feeling of being alone

left the old soul at eternity,

in hell, on earth,

only to make the journey

of rebirth

March 9, 2015

A child

Spells of wonder and enchantment
embody a child's soul,
lost and worry follow the passion
which burns within a whole
of a heart beating
against a box closing in
leaving and fleeting
the sensation inside a Bin.

2011

Groups

Thoughts echo outside

as sounds erupt,

leaving alliances divided

by a corrupt society unable to reach an understanding

of each individually distinct quality

without looking

at age, color, gender, size, class

only to silence speech

in order to pass

the message

of 'everything has labels'

with that puts a stop

to the reality

that we made those labels

2012

Equality

Spiteful people
with closed minds,
only to have a beadle
crawl behind
trying to pry
what was left behind
in a quake
of the eye,
to break
the cry, to nag
of equality which holds truth,
human decency,
acceptance,
and all the imperfection
that comes with it
equally.
To see work and sweat,
to see same-sex,
to see passed color, identity, class, gender
and all the stereotypes.
To erase the idea of the word color,
to see people as only people,
for who they are and not what society
constructed,
good and bad,

to see people without the perception of the media

and Popular culture.

To see peace,

to see love as love,

an eye blinded to shape or size,

no guidance in choice, but...

To see only God.

2012

Only human

Mental illness is a state of mind
only to the blind.
The struggle remains,
with the pain of being human,
each step is a victory
in the booming
ways of society
to see, to feel,
to open up ourselves
to the reality
come to think of it,
we are all human and just trying to make it

2012

Evolution

In the race of humans,
Who can play the part?
The part of many
hearts racing,
body aching,
separation,
existing,
plaguing,
playing,
taunting,
haunting,
feeding and finding my soul
only to leave sadness
in its wake,
so close,
so far,
humanity at its worst
only seeing A difference,
different,
same,
separated,
people choose separation

2012

Hope

As our wings take flight
For a journey into our heart
To find that one glittering star
That brightens up our night
Storms of lightning and rain
Fall on us
But we fight through them
Through it isn't easy
Finally e break out of the storm
To a shining golden light
Tears of joy fall down our neck
For the journey was worth it
We made it

2002

Death

Can be a scary thing for
some, yet a blessing for others.
The depth of the unknown
is a curious thing to say
the least of those who have
left this earth only to come back again,
having a story
to share,
To impart,
to share with those afraid
of death and what may come.
Others speak of flames, gnashing, and guilt
only to spend eternity
in their own hell
before returning
to a middle ground on earth,
change tends to happen
if only this knowledge
of mortality could change the world,
maybe everyone would
have a chance to find their peace.
Before one can imagine,
Life comes to an end.

2012

Innocent

The heart beat of a child's soul keeps pumping for air

For with out it the child is gone.

Yet inside that child's heart is not just the need to breathe

But to make a difference in this world.

This is the innocent child's wish in life,

To make a difference and be a peacemaker.

For there is more to life than back stabbing, making fun of people

And having the blood of hate in our veins.

For the blood of hate ill only turn darker

As life goes on.

So instead, the child would like pure golden blood to pass

On to others before heavens call her to peace and light.

For when the child meets the heavens she shall not feel the

Pain on earth anymore, but the warm touch of

God's hands.

2003

I wrote this poem when I was going through a hard time, but didn't want to give up on myself and my dreams. The girl is me in this poem.

My Hands

My hands were made

To make plans

In the shade

With a pen

And paper

To say amen

To the heavens

For the blessings

That exist

Everyday

In the midst

Of Gray
Of the day
Only to say
I Love you

8/18/2020

My Heart

There lays a child yearning to love in full bloom

In the rebirth of June

Love on the mind

Love is a kind

Act coming from my heart

Into your soul

Only to start

A passion of the whole

World

Spreading endless love

Hiding curled

Under the bedsheets

Only to rise

To the truth you are loved.

9/3/2020

Black Lives Matter

As the chatter
Of what truly matters
Is being publicized
Only to be advised
To be silent
When Black lives matter
Until then I will speak
I will stand
I will join in the voices
Speaking truth
Black Lives Matter
Isn't it time to make the changes?
That are being voiced everyday.
Black Lives Matter

9/19/2020

Finding Myself

A Perspective

Another person's perspective can be many things:
Sometimes, it can be as dark as night.
Other times, as bright as daylight.

Yet, when you look at someone else's perspective,
you're not only looking at their thoughts,
You're looking at the depths of their hearts
which tells who they really are.

January 2002

Judgment

As the stars glow at night
with no care on where it falls,
Sparkling with glee
with happiness while the other
consumed with dark judgment.

To stare only at humans who judge,
and to see a tear of blood may
teach us what pain judgment can inflict.

March 2002

Waiting Room

Surgery spells
and wishing wells
rise in a seldom crowded room.
Dreams flurry below too soon
as singing erupts
silently in the subtle interruptions.

In the midst
of confusion,
Is a world that has faith
mixed with weariness.

February 2017

Work Space

Different energies,
changing tides,
different creativity
filling every cravats,
finding side,
bringing memories
of a simpler time,
which guides
the mind
to find
one's
place.

March 21 2017

Pain

Burning pain,
endless tears,
emotional drain,
awaiting the mending
of a heart
shattered by the fallout,
in the art and act
of repression.

March 22, 2017

The Riddle of Life

Hidden pain,
forgotten words
inside a grain
eaten by a bluebird.

Life's a mystery
within a shell
of human history.

Bursting light
and darkness
in the flight
that awaits the stillness
of quietness.

May 2017

Hope

As our wings take flight
for a journey into our heart,
to find that one glittering star
that brightens up our night,
storms of lightning and rain
fall down on us,
but we fight through them
despite how hard it is.
Finally, we break out of the storm
to a shining golden light,
Tears of joy fall down on our necks
Due to the journey
We've accomplished.
We are glad to finally say finally,
"We made it through the illusion to hope"

September 9, 2002

Child's Play

Crows a bliss with bliss
as the city roar of the day.
Play a mist
of the say,
words of mouth
we are with God
to play as one
in two bodies
partners for eternity

June 22, 2018

Reflection

Looking within myself
only to find time,
only to see myself,
to be aligned,
to be defined,
to be refined,
to be kind,
to be designed
in two bodies,
only to find love.

July 30, 2018

Lost

Fire blazing within
an unforgettable soul:
trembling,
falling, and
losing control.

What was?
What will be…?
Nothing in hand.
Nothing!

Trembling,
finding,
searching,
up and down.

Hope lost
in translation.
July 2017

This Is Me

If you knew the real me,
without sin and only a grin.
Would you still be with me
or hide
as we have been?
Our truth is known to all,
only to heal inside and all.

We are manifestos,
we own our worth,
we are one.
In union,
no doubt
just love.

August 15, 2018

The Redemption

San Padro Sunkin City

Falling rocks
cliffs steep as hell
echoes of talking
with smell of cannabis
in the air
separating into the sea
only to find
the carefree
graffiti art
to mind
to heart
of the town

April 17, 2018

3

My mind speaks
to my heart
only to embody the soul.
The art of the goal
is to embrace from within,
forget the past
and let go of what has been.

July 26, 2018

Dr. MD, MD

Stretching between
the soulish and physical,
there lies growth
that's not your own.
A choice is to be made:
of life or leaving
this body
for a new one.

September 9, 2018

Dedicated to a doctor/teacher that taught me a lot in a small increment of time on my journey.

Healing

Knives of hate burrow into an innocent heart,
winds of confusion blow all-around a helpless body,
words of sweet sorrow embrace the soul
from the one that once loved.
The black sea covers the eyes only,
cloudy for the time ahead.
Only time will tell when and how long until it heals.

2004

Habit

As feelings of emotion
run through our veins
like a rapid river,
our hearts tremble
with a piece of enchantment
about to burst with drops of goodness,
yet there is one thing holding us back:
Our habit of hurting others
with word's attitude,
and the only way to stop that habit
is to keep the golden riches of love in our hearts.
Then, maybe someday, the habit will be forgotten.

2003

The Eyes of a Painter

Gazing at a blank canvas,

brushes are lying next to colors of every kind.

Knowledge and feelings imprisoned within

soon become part of the canvas.

Blue and black hues mix with each stroke,

an image begins to arise.

With each detail, new colors are introduced,

with each color, new things are made to be Conceived

Making what was once nothing into something meaningful.

Yet the person who can understand it's significance

is the one who made the painting come to life.

2000

The awakening

Letting Go

Did as I was told:
got to let it flow
and trust the tow
of the universe,
which is my soul;
My soul
at the core,
healing with me.
I've got to find self-love,
to make a foundation
of a union of love—
Endless unconditional love.

August 24, 2018

Healing Hands

Ever-flowing,
Healing,
Exploding,
Changing,
Teaching,
Growing
to find your own
self
in the absence of sound
of realization,
of the power,
of love.

August 26, 2018

The Road Less Traveled

Beaten and bruised, I take
the road less traveled,
forgotten and grown over,
grown over and less spoken of,
I take the road less traveled.
Many who have walked on
the road less traveled in the past,
now left, only to
be forever forgotten.

I take the road less traveled,
which is different in every way.
I tread the road less traveled—
It's the path that's dreaded.
I take the road less traveled,
though, in reality, it's a piece
of what was a part of me.
It feels good to be there,
as I take the road less traveled.

March 2015

Redemption

Waves from the past
brush the present
with hope
to make a last
conversation meant
to piece together
what was broken,
to cope
and redeem
each piece,
weaving
each wave back
as one.
The redemption,
the freedom,
sing as one
with the waves.

January 12, 2016

Calico

Sensations of hope,

visions of a white phoenix, holding a rope

embodies a female

with paws and fur,

a heart of purity.

Deception Plays songs of lies

dancing here and there,

only to see past it,

a rise of what's true

stays,

plays

for days

and keeps the feline alive.

January 15, 2016

2 P's

Two Pisces intuitively drawn
to guide,
to connect,
to share
gifts of their own.
To learn,
to grow
and give growth
for we are one—
one mind, one source of consciousness,

September 1, 2018

Looks

It can be deceiving.
Never look a look
in the eye, you'd be lost
to reality.
The core
is in the essence,
the truth,
who we are?
as one.

September 1, 2018

Unconditional love

Myself

It upsets me I walked away
without even a second glance,
I thought we had a chance,
had to go deep inside
to find you were
there
all along,
lurking,
I just had to shed
the rules of society
and its anxiety
to lead me back to you.

July 22, 2018

One

No matter how bleak,
seeing my true self
through the same soul
with hazel eyes in oneself,
to feel truly whole,
to stay aligned,
to embrace the light
from within,
to fight
and begin,
to spread
love and peace
to everyone.

August 11, 2018

Home

Heart of home
is where people
exist
only to be restraint
in
fear
of lies.
God is strength
and home
there is only love
and constant
safety.
God is love
to remembering
you are loved.

4/23/19

DJ Jane

Bass, House plays
as dancers play
as one
in a large gathering
of divine brothers and sisters
to love
to learn
to grow
to dance as one
on the dance floor

2/24/19

Surrender

When the world
around me
seems to be crumbling
it's only making
room
for
life's
growth
an abundance
prayers
being answered
learning to live
by
faith
by
love
and trusting myself
each
step of
the way.

4/24/19

Freedom

Awakening to freedom
surrendering
to the truth of God
with his
unconditional love
connecting and remembering
what was and has
always been
God
love
eternal

1/28/19

Completely Unknown

Following the good feeling

even as fear

comes to lie

the truth always prevails

love

is the truth

there is no fear

just

love

as the path opens

things become clearer

surrenders

to the flow

4/26/19

Foundation

Early morning
days
of leaving
work
only to return
under God's protection
following my heart
in dreams becoming a reality
always moving forward
trusting each step
always hidden gems
in the unknown

5/7/19

Quit space

Unexpected time off without WIFI
little light
can be seen as a burden
it's a gift
to follow the steps
given from the divine
God's plan
taking place
no control
following
the flow

5/10/19

Thrill of Unknown

Is but a sign
of deeper love
plunging
spreading
expanding
showing the truth
within
that we are all one
and only love is real

2/27/19

God's Dynasty

Diamonds shine their light
of love
on a ring finger
the birth of marriage
that always was
between two
lifetime lovers
formed from same soul
emerging to heal
false messages
and the lies we tell ourselves
to be fully back
where we have always
been
is love.

2/2/19

Seeding

Planting a seed
of love
in the false lies
only to break free
and see
the truth
that only love
remains
that love
has never
left or
abandoned
you
Love remains in
wanting
everything you
want
just keep going

5/21/19

Peace

Is found within
nothing outside
can harm
or diminish
the peace
that has been
and always will be
healing each
what has been engrained
in our hearts
only to lead
to truth
you are loved

5/21/19

Growth in Change

Changing waves
being pulled
to heavens
feast
as
love
is the way
in every direction
love is the way
it will be the change
as you grow
to understand
you have always been loved
and dreams are meant to
work in your favor
10/10/2019

God's Love

In every chaotic moment of life
God is and was always loving
Me and everyone
where I needed to see clearer
and see myself as a whole
and see the truth
that I am so loved
and worthy of my good
which is within and all around
the gift
of all his children
light of the world
gifts from God
can
only
spread like fire
until lies
no longer is scene
or has a voice
lies
will be silenced
with love
with God
with life
with the truth of love
5/25/19

Trust

Learning to trust me
Rooted in a relationship with God
always showing me the way
in every moment
even when doubt arises
only to be diminished by the truth—
love
the only real thing
the rest a mirage
meant to be healed
healing is key
on a journey of love

5/29/19

God's truth

Truth lies within
of every brother and sister
the soul quaking
and shaking
being molded to the truth
of who I have always
been a lover
friend
teacher
poet
writer
influencer
entertainer
lover of God
God unconditionally teaching me about myself
as I get to know his truth and his love
as we are all love as God is love.

6/4/19

Heaven

Heaven must be a wonderful place

Where people come from every race

Where there are people of every face

God brings His hand down to bring somebody

New to heaven.

God loves everybody

It does not matter how you look or from

Where you came because in God's eye's

We are all the same

Fall 1999

Christmas Prayer

May your Christmas be filled with family and all the ones you
Love,
May life take you through a journey of hope and give you the
Willpower,
To never-give up, even when it seems as though there is no
Hope.
May you learn more and more about your inner
Beauty.
May you follow your heart to wherever it brings you.
May
Your life be filled with all the love a person can
Hold
All the friends and family a person can handle.
All
The faith, hope, and light, a person can only dream of,
And
May you always remember your golden heart that shines
Inside and out.

December 2004

Truth

In turmoil, there is nothing
Just to feel and heal
leads to a real
result
change of perspective
all things are possible
surrendering
to the constant flow
each relationship deepening
further in
love and to love him
is all God wants,
is always loving you

6/11/19

Standing in my truth

God calling me to stand in my truth
as a leader
influencer
boss
writer
author
entertainer
all words that are love
and how God created me
and to not believe in the lies
but to stand in my truth.

6/12/19

31

Age is timeless
it means nothing
we are all God's children
of infinite youth and love
celebrating another success
and upgrade in life
with God
being with God
trusting and surrendering
having the relationship and life
I always dreamed
being thankful for all
the gifts
God gives daily
In the form
Of unconditional love

6/14/2019

Falling apart

God holds you through everything
as changes occur
it feels like the end of the world
that is never true
God asking is with you
in everyone and everything
just love yourself and care for others the rest will follow

6/20/19

Stability

God is the foundation
the truth
the way
to never give up no matter what
trust in God trust in self
God is beside all his children
just love
and allow love to flow from within

6/20/19

Ebb and Flow

Flow
flowing through
the chaos
of a never-ending cycle of love
unexpected gifts and miracles
always constant
God-loving me through it
all

6/21/19

Miracle

When all seems lost it's not
cause you can't lose love
God always showing you
places to love yourself and others
with that
makes room for miracles
trusting and surrendering
no matter what the illusion
looks like
to be in harmony with God
is to overcome my fears
that have been built up
in your heart
and release them
and let go

6/26/19

Honoring life

Dancing to the rhythm of life
Is only a strife
Away from finding true love
With the heavens above
Shining joy
On everyone to enjoy
The blessing
Of expressing
Oneself through creating
By stating
One love

9/17/2020

Recommended Materials

Who you are a children's book by Jessi Hersey

Journey through Heart songs by Mattie J.T. Stepanek

Complete Sonnets and Poems: The Oxford Shakespeare complete Sonnets and Poems 2008

4. Loving thoughts by Helena Steiner Rice

Follow on Social media

Instagram: @Jeasih10

Facebook: @Jeasih10

Twitter: @Jeasih10

The company Facebook page: @Onenesslovepublishing

Twitter: @1nesslove

Instagram: 1nesslove123

The poetry book Facebook page: @litsoul

You can explore services in coaching in publishing here: www.1nesslove.com

<u>The End</u>